Overcome Anxiety

Rewire Your Brain Using Neuroscience & Therapy Techniques to Overcome Anxiety, Depression, Fear, Panic Attacks, Worry, and Shyness: In Social Meetings, Relationships, at Work, and More

Lilly Andrew

Table of Contents

Table of Contents
Introduction
Chapter 1: The Science of Fear and Anxiety

- The Neuroscience of Fear and Anxiety
- The Power of Cognitive-Behavioral Approach to Anxiety
- What is Cognitive Behavioral Approach?
- How to Identify the Cause of Your Anxiety

Chapter 2: Anxiety in Four Life Areas and How to Handle It

- Anxiety in Relationships
- Work-Related Anxiety
- Social Anxiety
  - How a 27-Year-Old Man Became Social Phobia-Free in 15 Weeks
- Family-Related Anxiety

Chapter 3: What to Do to Stay On Top of Your Mental Health

- Know Yourself
- Changing Your Habits
- How to Handle Fear
  - How to Annihilate Negative Thoughts
- Learn to Relax Your Body
- Controlling Your Breath
- Improve Your Self-Confidence
- How to Handle a Panic Attack

Conclusion

Introduction

"People have asked me many times to speak before a group, but I have not been able to do so. The problem is that I get nervous and my mind freezes and turns blank, so I have avoided it all through my life. But now, I am a manager and I must run various kinds of meetings and apply for funding of projects from our company's finance committee. I simply have to do a great deal of talking. I'm not sure if it's really possible to get rid of this anxiety I feel when the thought of speaking to groups come to mind." These were Peter's words sharing his concerns with his friend Mike. It is certainly not a good space to be in, and unfortunately, there are many people who suffer from a variety of anxieties.

It is for this reason that I wrote this book: to help people like you live normal lives and experience the joy of life on this planet. The focus of this book is not merely to give you actionable steps to practice, but also it is to provide the theory behind why the actions are effective.

The book begins with looking into the neuroscience of fear and anxiety. These two emotions are almost the same because the same brain circuits are activated, and the body experiences similar reactions. But, the two differ slightly because the threats that trigger them aren't immediate in both situations. After this, we delve into a method that has proved effective in healing various kinds of anxiety. You'll learn about the story of a 27-year-old Indian man who had a social phobia and couldn't even leave his home. However, through the method we will share in chapter 1, this man was able get rid of his mental health issue and, he even expanded the organization for which he was working.

Chapter 2 goes into detail about the anxiety in the workplace, in social settings, with family, and in relationships. A 2019 article on Psychreg reveals that the UK government reported that, in 2017-2018, they found that 595,000 employees were suffering from work-related stress, depression, and anxiety. It further said that 15.4 million working days were lost due to these mental health issues. Not only do we talk about these, but we also show you the various ways you can deal with each one of them. You'll also discover a mental error that most of us fall victim to and how to avoid it.

In the last chapter, we go at length on selected ideas that help you stay on top of your mental health. We begin by talking about the value of knowing yourself. This is so vital, and we show you some things you can do to begin this self-knowledge process. Really, how do you manage your health better if you've yet to figure out what gets your life juices flowing? The other topic we discuss is the importance of being able to alter your habits. This helps you grab the reins of your life and create it the way you want. Isn't that exciting? Imagine creating any habit that will enable you, not only to prevent anxiety, but also to achieve the kind of goals about which you've always dreamt! We also explain what a panic attack is and how to manage it.

Anxiety is not something to take lightly because it can ruin your whole life. So, if you really would like to take charge of your life and mental health, you have no time to waste! Turn the pages of this book, and find out how to grab anxiety by the scruff of its neck and strangle it to death, once for all. Let's start with the first chapter right away.

Chapter 1: The Science of Fear and Anxiety

A man was jogging one day, and his eyes flashed on an object on the left side of the road. Immediately, his heart rate skyrocketed, his breathing frequency increased, and he began to sweat profusely. At the same time, he instantly stopped, zoomed in on the object, and realized that it was an old car tire laying on its side in the green grass. What had happened to the man was that he went into fear mode, and his body was preparing either to run, to fight, or to freeze. Fortunately, he brought in the help of the executive part of the brain, called the cortex, to evaluate, objectively, what he thought was the threat. This is an example of fear. So, fear is an emotion that you feel when faced with an immediate threat forcing the body to switch into survival mode. How does it differ from anxiety? The difference is really about timing. The next story helps show what anxiety is.

A friend of mine had a girlfriend who, one day, disappeared from home. When my friend asked the woman's sister where his girlfriend was, she said that she had gone with her friend to some city about 50 miles away. That night, my friend did not sleep. He was deep in thoughts trying to figure out if indeed his girl had gone to the city or not. The following morning, my friend went to work, but he could not concentrate on his job. He was worried and anxious that his girlfriend might have gone to cheat on him. Eventually, he asked his boss if he could go early, and he got permission. I'll cut this story here because it enables us to define what anxiety is. In this case, the threat my friend "saw" was his girlfriend cheating. His thoughts dwelt on this possibility until his body chemistry changed so much that he could not sleep. This is anxiety. It is an emotion that you feel when worried about a threat that may only be in your mind or in the future. This statement sums up the major way anxiety occurs, "when we speak of the cortex pathway to anxiety, we're generally focused on interpretations, images, and worries that the cortex creates, or on anticipatory thoughts that create anxiety when no danger is present" Pittman, 2015, p.20).

What happens within our brains when we enter into the fear or anxiety mode? Science has the answer.

The Neuroscience of Fear and Anxiety

Fear and anxiety are both emotions and come about as a result of activation of the part of the brain called the amygdala. This little organ is almond-shaped and there are two, with one located on each half of the brain called the hemisphere. The amygdala is linked with both the thalamus and the cortex. The large convoluted part of the brain that is in contact with the skull is what is called the cortex. I should mention here that the brain's parts are interlinked in a complex network that science hasn't yet been able to identify all of them. The thalamus distributes sensory information from the environment either directly to the amygdala or through the cortex.

The amygdala is often seen as the organ of fear because it triggers behaviors associated with emotion. How does fear occur? When your senses (eyes, ears, nose, skin, or tongue) pick up a stimulus from the environment, they send it to the amygdala through the thalamus. The amygdala houses emotional memories that people learnt from their past experiences. When a sensory signal enters the amygdala, which in turn quickly checks if there's immediate danger or not, based on past experience, by using the law of association. Some of our emotional memories don't come from our own experiences but are wired into the brain right from birth.

The cortex is inefficient in activating the body to respond to a threat. The problem with the cortex is that it takes time to think things through, and in the presence of real danger, you might be killed. So, it makes absolute sense for the amygdala to override the cortex. But, this fear organ can also act erroneously by assuming some things pose an immediate threat even if they don't. For example, to other people's amygdalas, the eyes of people watching them when they're about to speak in public may pose a threat. Perhaps they do, but in many cases, the worst thing that can happen is that these people could laugh at you, not kill you.

The amygdala, when it perceives an immediate threat, triggers the release hormones such as epinephrine (adrenaline) that initiate physiological changes such as a spike in heart rate. These changes prepare the body either to fight, to freeze, or to run so that you can remain alive. Therefore, fear can be important when rightfully triggered, but it can also be unfounded. Hence, there is a need to understand what fear is and how to handle it.

Anxiety, on the other hand, occurs via two pathways that science has discovered. One is the exact one described above on fear. The key difference is that the source of the threat doesn't pose immediate danger. You may hear the news that you are going to be laid off in two months' time. This information might trigger past thoughts and emotions when you had no job and battled to make ends meet. Dwelling on these thoughts may eventually trigger anxiety about the whole situation. However, if you had to think about the situation from the cortex-perspective, using your reasoning ability, you may find that you being laid off is a great opportunity in disguise. For example, you may have the opportunity to work for a company that better uses your strengths, and thus, it would provide you with work that you enjoy. But, it can only be an opportunity if you look for a seed of greater benefit.

The second neural pathway, of anxiety, involves the cortex. It's important to note that the amygdala receives the sensory signals much faster than the cortex for swift action in case of danger. Hence, most therapists focus their attention on the cortex path because the origins of anxiety are not necessarily a threat. The cortex part of the brain is responsible for high-order functions such as reasoning, analyzing, and mathematics. It helps when you evaluate danger. Here's how it plays a role in anxiety; the sense organs, like with fear, pick up stimuli and pass them onto the thalamus. Upon receiving this information, the thalamus sends the signal to various parts of the cortex for processing and interpretation. Processed information is sent to the other parts of the brain, especially the frontal lobe, to help you perceive and understand the stimuli. The frontal lobe is located just behind your forehead and the eyes. It is the largest lobe in the human brain, and it's also larger than those in animals. This major part of the brain has the ability to predict the future, and its consequences, make plans, solve problems, handle what-if scenarios, and therefore, it can easily anticipate things turning bad.

But, it's most important job is in directing our thoughts to conduct our lives in a way suggested by Sadhguru, an Indian mystic, when he said, "The only thing that stands between you and your well-being is a simple fact: you have allowed your thoughts and emotions to take instruction from the outside rather than the inside" (Sadhguru, 2016, p.20).

Because of the power to foretell, the frontal lobe can make you into a worrier by focusing your mind on thoughts of concern. It's perhaps vital to state here that worry is a phenomenon that occurs at a mental level when focused on what could go wrong; while, anxiety is an emotion you feel within the body through reactions such as heart palpitations. Your worries can be so serious that they begin to interfere with your daily life, and this condition is termed "generalized anxiety disorder."

The Power of Cognitive-Behavioral Approach to Anxiety

Two men were once laid off from their jobs on the same day. They were still young, both these men, at just over 30 years of age. Seeing that they still had a lot of life ahead of them, they began to pound the streets looking for jobs. For 6 whole months, they got nothing but a series of rejection letters. Finally, one of the men stopped searching for work, and he spent his days binge-watching television and drinking lots of beer.

One day, he woke up early in the morning and got ready for what looked like another go at job hunting. His wife was elated. This young man took his wife to work and the children to school. He then came back home, locked himself in the garage and left the car

engine running and took his young life. The other man kept going and eventually, after 8 months, he got a job. Let's analyze what happened with the young man who terminated his life and left his children fatherless:
- Event – He got rejection after rejection.
- Dominant thoughts – He began to think that he would never get a job no matter how long he looked. He further felt small for being taken care of by his wife.
- Emotions and body reactions– Dejected, stressed, hopeless, and headaches.
- Behavior – Watched unlimited television, drank lots of beer, and finally committed a suicide.

This is indeed a sad story that should never have happened had the young man knew of the cognitive behavioral approach to anxiety. The process this therapy follows could have helped pick out the core issues and helped the young man address them. In the interest of saving lives and helping others lead healthy lives, let's look closer at cognitive behavioral approach to mental and health issues.

What is Cognitive Behavioral Approach?

Cognitive Behavioral Approach is the kind of therapy that believes that cognition (thinking) affects behavior and can be monitored and changed. Further, this approach suggests that you can change your thoughts to affect desired behaviors. It became an important therapy from the 1960s when psychologists and therapists began to adopt the role of thoughts in emotions and actions. This is interesting because past civilizations had known about the impact of thoughts on character and conduct. We know this because some of them shared with us ways to attain qualities such as self-control. In fact, James Allen (n.d.) once said that the first step to become a person of self-control was to introspect, to look within. Here's what he said in his own words, "Introspection. This coincides with the observation of the natural scientist. The mental eye is turned like a searchlight upon the inner things of the mind, and its subtle and ever varying processes are observed and carefully noted. This stepping aside from selfish gratifications, from the excitements of worldly pleasures and ambitions, in order to observe, with the object of understanding, one's nature, is the beginning of self-control. Hitherto, the man has been blindly and impotently borne along by the impulses of his nature, the mere creature of things and circumstances, but now he puts a check upon his impulses and, instead of being controlled, begins to control" (Allen, n.d., p.309).

The difference between what Allen says and the cognitive behavioral approach is that the latter utilizes the service of the therapist to help you turn inward and watch the role thoughts play in your behavior. Hence, this approach depends largely on the active collaboration of the therapist and the patient. The core goal is to help the patient to identify the thoughts that trigger and contribute to emotions such as anxiety. It is a guided discovery and requires a therapist who's an expert on working with people. Such a therapist needs to be patient, caring, empathetic, and be a great listener who asks quality questions like a good detective. The main reason that you may need a therapist is because some of your thoughts can escape your awareness while still causing you anxiety. But, a cognitive behavioral approach-trained therapist can help you find and evaluate those thoughts that trigger anxiety and worry.

In this book however, we want you to become your own cognitive behavioral approach therapist. Perhaps you may be thinking, "Does this approach work?" To answer you, let me take you to a research study that took place to establish if cognitive behavioral therapy (CBT) works compared to a placebo. The latter is a group of people who are used as a control in a research or experiment so that an unbiased comparison can be made. In this case, Stephan Hofmann, PhD., and Jasper Smits, PhD. (2008) conducted a meta-analysis study to figure out the efficacy of cognitive behavioral therapy versus placebo for adults with a variety of anxiety disorders such as social anxiety. To that end, these two researchers screened 1,165 people and found that only 27 met their exacting study criteria. The selected studies had a total of 1,496 patients. After careful analysis, Hofmann and Smits discovered that cognitive behavioral therapy produced great results for the patients as opposed to a placebo. This led them to conclude in their own words, "CBT yields significantly greater benefits than placebo treatments" (Hofmann and Smits, 2008, p.6). So, the question shouldn't be whether the cognitive behavioral approach works or not; the focus should be on following the process as close as possible and doing the exercises suggested. Only then could you know whether this therapy works for you or not. You hold the key to whether you recover from anxiety through this process or not.

How to Identify the Cause of Your Anxiety

You never want anxiety therapy unless you feel it is needed. So, people who go to cognitive behavioral therapy are usually in a hopeless and overwhelmed situation. Their main problem is that they aren't sure as to what is the cause of their anxiety. Hence, the major step to take is first to understand what are the major factors to anxiety. Then, you can go to the root cause of anxiety, and cut it off. Treating only the symptoms, such as using medication, has never brought any lasting results. It's like when you want to kill weeds; do you cut off the leaves, branches, or roots? Obviously, you go after the roots. So it is with anxiety. The roots must be severed for lasting positive results. Now, what are the roots? Let's retrace our footsteps and look at the story of the man who killed himself after failing to get a job.

We know he killed himself, and that's the behavior he took after he felt he couldn't handle his body reactions and emotions. Why did his body react the way it did? Simply because that young man dwelt on thoughts of hopelessness which eventually necessitated the body to react drastically in order to release the tension. Unfortunately, the body usually does this by causing ailments. So, the pains we feel in our bodies are a sign that something in our brain isn't right. Hence, the roots the young man could have annihilated were his negative and paralyzing automatic thoughts. The cognitive behavioral approach to anxiety seeks to identify these sorts of thoughts that result in the anxiety you feel. Sadhguru confirmed this when he said, "But if you look at this carefully and with absolute sincerity, you will realize that the way you think is the way you feel" (Sadhguru, 2016, p.191). One big question to ask is, "What is the origin of automatic thoughts, and what are they?"

Automatic thoughts occur subconsciously without your awareness. They generally originate from the entrenched beliefs that guide your life. All of us get programmed, from childhood, with certain ideas, and the process continues throughout life. Some of the beliefs are created by ourselves as we grow older. These beliefs are our references when we have to make snap decisions. For example, if you're walking in the woods and all of sudden you see a bear, what happens? If you were raised with a belief that a bear is dangerous, and can kill humans, then you'll very likely run or be ready to protect yourself, right? But someone who believes a bear isn't dangerous would most probably watch the bear and never even think about running. This example illustrates how our beliefs affect how we think and eventually act.

In summary, you begin the therapeutic process by identifying exactly how you feel. Your emotions of anxiety are the key to access your mind and find the cause. This is why James Allen spoke about introspection as the first step to intelligent self-control. Here, your introspection seeks to spot the exact feelings and eventually, the corresponding automatic thoughts you're experiencing. Once you spot the thoughts that are responsible for producing the anxiety, your next step is to change these thoughts. If you don't change these thoughts, then you cannot expect your anxiety to go away because the root isn't upended. The big question now is, "How do I change my negative thoughts to positive once I've identified them?"

The answer, you'll realize, is a relatively simple one, but some people sneer at it. The way to change your thoughts is exactly the way you formed them into beliefs in the first place. The principle that you used to install those beliefs in your mind is called "suggestion." Basically, this principle works by exposing your mind to a specific idea over and over again until it is wired into your brain and body. However, for most of us, these beliefs originated from other people, not us. Unfortunately, some do not serve us, like the automatic negative thoughts that may create anxiety.

To illustrate how to turn your negative thoughts into positive, building ones, let's say that your negative thought says, "Only qualified people get good jobs," which blocks you from applying for a good vacancy. To neutralize this thought, you can create an idea such as this: "I've done good jobs in the past for which I started with no qualifications. It is not the qualification which is important, but the skills to do the job. I want this kind of a job, and I will learn the skills and get this job." Now, you write this statement on a card, and you read it over and over again, especially in the morning and before you sleep at night. At these times, your awareness is slightly low, and it is easier to access the subconscious and reprogram it.

Chapter 2: Anxiety in Four Life Areas and How to Handle It

We have already seen that anxiety by itself isn't a bad thing when at reasonable levels. However, the moment it interferes with other aspects of life such as work, it can be a problem. In this chapter, we will talk about four areas where anxiety can cause problems and learn how to handle this mental issue in such situations. The areas to consider are social anxiety, work-related anxiety, anxiety in relationships, and family-related anxiety. Let's go over each of them.

Anxiety in Relationships

Romantic relationships require openness for them to be healthy and enjoyable for both partners. Unfortunately, when you're open, you run the risk of being hurt or even attract disappointments. Uncertainty is one element common in many anxiety situations. It's no wonder in romantic relationships that insecurity is such a big factor in anxiety. People with social anxiety or generalized anxiety may find it a challenge to manage their relationships. Some people may not be aware that they're facing relationship anxiety. The answers to these questions may be of help if you are not sure.

- Do you try as hard as you can to avoid tough conversations with your partner?
- Do you often feel anxious when your partner has gone shopping, to a workshop, work, or out with friends?
- Do you often worry that your partner may be cheating on you?

If you have answered any of the above questions with a yes, you may be experiencing relationship anxiety. There are guides you can follow to handle relationship anxiety. Let's go over four of them.

- **Avoid labelling your partner.** Some people have a tendency to describe their partner by using one-word-descriptions such as "He's insecure," or "She's disrespectful," and many others. Is there a person who can be fully described by just one quality? Think about this for a moment and you'll see that any person has a multitude of qualities. But, once you describe them in one word, you're giving your brain a directive to look for that quality in your partner regularly. And, guess what? You won't be disappointed because your brain will direct your senses to spot the quality. Like everyone else, you have blindspots; and therefore, you should practice tolerance. As you do so, you can tactfully bring to the attention of your partner any negative quality you spot and help deal with it intelligently. Most importantly, try as best as you could to deal with facts instead of opinions, and your spouse will appreciate your help, and thus you both will build a better functioning relationship.

- **Eliminate the tendency to blame your partner**. No one is without fault whether we are aware of it or not. The problem is that we usually don't take kindly to being blamed even when we know that we are at fault. When someone blames you, don't you feel the urge to defend yourself? Most people do. So, blaming isn't the best way to deal with issues in relationships. Rather, first investigate the role you may have played or avoided in the relationship problem both of you may be facing. You may be surprised to find that you were the cause of the problem in the first place. Even if your partner may be responsible, you still have to treat her with respect and focus on dealing with issues instead of the person. Most importantly, remember that the way you deal with issues in your romantic relationship usually mirrors how you handle other kinds of connections as well.

- **Scrutinize your thinking**. Have you ever found yourself thinking that your partner is planning to leave you? If so, you have fallen into the trap of what's called "cognitive distortions." These are basic thinking patterns that we erroneously fall into; although, in many cases, they are wrong. Thinking your partner is planning to leave you is an example of a mind reading distortion. Is it really possible to know exactly what another person is thinking unless you're a psychic? The best way to deal with this kind of cognitive distortion is simply to ask your partner if you suspect something untoward about them. Also, turn the searchlight into your own thoughts, and you'll likely find that your own core beliefs and ideas are the culprit.

- **Identify and follow your personal interests**. Romantic relationships are just one element that make up a complete life. Too much focus on yours may sooner or later exhume some things you don't like. It is not a bad thing to focus on the strengths of the relationship, but do remember that imperfections turn diamonds into sparkling gems. One good way to lower relationship anxiety is to pursue your personal goals and interests. In fact, according to Kathleen Smith, PhD, (n.d.) people who boast strong relationships and put energy into achieving their personal goals and interests are more likely to make better partners. By the way, your partner may have been attracted to you because they saw you working on your goals and knew you're the kind they'd like to spend the rest of their life with.

Work-Related Anxiety

A young woman was once employed at a copper-producing company. One of her tasks, every month's end, was to do a stock take and then prepare a metal accounting report. This task required her to make lots of estimates from month to month, and this frustrated her very much. Over a period of time, this woman began to hate this task, and for some reason, she managed to stay on the task for a few years. But, after her maternity leave, she declined to do the task reasoning that it stresses her out. You can be sure that his lady didn't enjoy the accounting task. But, she did it every month because of the support she got from her seniors, or else she would have avoided the task at all costs. This is what work-related anxiety and anxiety in general can do. According to Kathleen Smith, PhD, (n.d.) about 75% of people with anxiety or stress report that it negatively impacts their daily lives and work. Hence, it is important to identify and deal effectively with it.

Workplace anxiety is a major concern for both employers and workers because it impacts many work outcomes. For example, elevated anxiety at work can negatively impact the attitude and performance of employees. How do you tell if you may be a victim of work anxiety? There are a number of signs you can check for to diagnose yourself such as:

- Lower self-confidence
- When you are often pessimistic
- When you avoid setting goals and subsequently being unproductive
- When you give up easily when things get a bit tough
- Getting easily discouraged, which may lead to underperformance
- Poor work relationship with your colleagues
- Low social skills

At the workplace, anxiety may surface in a variety of ways such as social anxiety, generalized anxiety, or other kinds. People who are anxious tend to be dissatisfied with their jobs. It's not surprising considering that anxiety can lead to a drop in job performance and cause you to take less risks and think less about the future and innovation. Not only does workplace anxiety kill creativity and initiative, but it can also make you despise your work. What are the major causes of anxiety?

There are several causes such as: deadlines, working with difficult people, unclear job descriptions, inconsiderate managers, ineffective communication amongst workers, lack of vision, poor relations with colleagues, and lack of fairness. The list of causes can go on and on because there are so many factors involved. If you find that you have work-related anxiety, how can you deal with it? There are a number of ways, and we discuss some below:

- **Create a personal wellness plan that includes sufficient sleep, eating healthy meals, exercising, and participating in social activities after work hours**. This plan will help you cope with the anxiety you feel while at work, but it does not get rid of it.
- **Improve your ways of dealing with your colleagues**. One major problem at work is gossip and office politics. The best way to deal with gossip is to face the specific person instead of talking about them with others. Gossiping only creates tension amongst employees and can hurt work productivity and fuel your anxiety.
- **Clarify your job role with your boss**. Certain roles have vague job descriptions. Even the ones with good job descriptions can be a problem because they're not followed. If you're the kind that thrives on structure, the lack of adherence and clarity on job roles can cause you anxiety. How? At one stage you're doing the job of an office manager, and, two hours later, you're expected to run a project meeting. Yet, you're employed as a software developer. Don't laugh; some companies lack structure to a point where you can wonder how they survive. Your recourse is to meet with your boss and together commit to an agreed job description as well as the expected deliveries.
- **Agree to realistic deadlines**. There are times when deadlines aren't negotiable. In such cases, the best route is to ask for concessions on some of the activities you may be doing so that you can focus on the emergency task. Where possible, always negotiate for a deadline that will allow you to do a good job instead of simply trying to please your boss by delivering in a hurry but shoddy work.
- **Deal in facts, not opinions**. One of the deadly issues at work is the habit of generalizing. It is far easier to do so

than to think accurately because the latter takes serious mental effort. But, if you resolve to deal in facts, then you'll find that others will be careful when they engage with you and will be more likely to avoid gossiping and offering unwelcome opinions.

Social Anxiety

Social anxiety is the anticipated fear of being negatively judged and evaluated by others. A common situation likely to initiate this kind of anxiety is public speaking. A research study by Dwyer and Davidson (2012) discovered that college students more often selected speaking to a group as their top fear. However, the same study found, the fear of death came out at the top with public speaking ranked third. So, the thought of speaking can cause some people to go into anxiety mode.

If you usually become anxious in social events and situations but are confident when you are alone, then you may be a victim of social anxiety. Many people suffer from either a specific social anxiety or generalized social anxiety. A specific social anxiety is the kind you only experience when you begin to think about doing a given activity such as public speaking. On the other hand, generalized social anxiety occurs when you're nervous and uncomfortable in a variety of social environments. Social anxiety may be triggered when: you are criticized, you are the center of attention, you are meeting people with authority such as a chief executive officer (CEO), or you are meeting strangers.

Typical symptoms of social anxiety include some of the following:

- A dry throat and mouth
- Increased heart rate
- Turning red, especially if you are of a lighter skin
- Difficulty swallowing

Social anxiety, like all other anxieties, can be a cause for concern when it affects your work, relationships, mental, and emotional health. For this reason, you need to find an effective treatment. One of the most powerful approaches to cure anxiety is the cognitive-behavioral approach we discussed in chapter 1. Here's how one person turned his life around through this therapy.

How a 27-Year-Old Man Became Social Phobia-Free in 15 Weeks

The story happened in India, and the protagonist was an unmarried man who earned an average income. This story is captured in a 2009 research by Priyamvada, R., Kumari, S., Prakash, J., and Chaudhury, S. Over a period of time, this man had begun to avoid crowds and preferred to stay at home. His inferiority complex had also finally caused him to lose interest in his work. Not surprisingly, he spent most of his time wallowing in thoughts of inadequacy, low self-esteem, and even showed signs of depression.

To his credit, this man went and sought help, and he got one in the form of cognitive behavioral therapy. The therapists, after initially building rapport and hearing his life story, determined the following therapy aims for him:
- To help him reduce his anxiety, inferiority complex, and improve his self-esteem
- To assist him in learning how to alter his automatic negative thoughts

The treatment took 17 sessions and spanned a total of 15 weeks. One of the key steps taken was first to teach this man how to breathe properly followed by tutoring him on how to relax his body and mind. Thereafter, the therapist educated him on how to challenge his unproductive, automatic, negative thoughts, and he also taught him to restructure his erroneous and inaccurate beliefs from childhood. After all was done, this protagonist got the following results:

- His anxiety and feelings of guilt subsided, while his self-esteem received a boost.
- Interestingly, he began to attend social gatherings.

The therapist made a follow up with him 6 months after the treatment and discovered that things were really going well. For example, the once-social anxiety sufferer had expanded the non-governmental organization (NGO) that he worked for to other cities. This case study concluded that a combination of cognitive, emotional, and behavioral treatments are effective in reversing social phobias.

Family-Related Anxiety

According to Dr. Samantha Rodman in her 2018 article "*Raised by anxious parents? Here's How it Might Be Affecting Your Mental Health*," it is insanely tough for a child who grows up with an anxious parent to live a joyful life. This is what family-related anxiety can do if not treated. You can imagine how challenging it would be for a child whose parents are both anxious. Perhaps this story illustrates better how an anxious parent can begin the process of "handing over" anxiety to their children.

Joyce was about to take her two little daughters to attend their dance classes. At the same time, she had a work assignment that needed to be completed right then because it had already been delayed. After finishing with the task, she discovered that her daughters hadn't yet put on their dance clothes. She felt a surge of adrenaline pumping in her blood as she felt overwhelmed and frustrated. Anyway, she got the girls to adorn their fancy clothes and got on the road with them in time. On the way while in the car, Joyce snapped, and she shouted at her little impressionable children for failing to wear their dance clothes on time. Her heart was racing hard as she did so. She had lost control, and luckily, she kept the car's wheels on the road. What's sad is that Joyce wasn't lashing out at her daughters for the time. It had been something she did a few times almost weekly. Hence, she had been trying to overcome her anxiety as fast as she could.

Now, here's the problem. Children see parents as their role models whether we are aware of it or not. Therefore, they copy a lot of what we do and how we do it. A few days ago, I saw a 7-year-old wearing her grandmother's shoes. When I asked her why, she shrugged and moved on. She did it for no other reason than to look like an adult and be like her granny. If there's anything, as parents, we should learn about our children, it is this: children are like a sponge and absorb a lot of what happens in their environment. Perhaps a quote by John B. Watson, the deceased behavioral psychologist, is in order here. He once said, "Give me a dozen healthy infants, well-formed, and my own specified world to bring them up in and I'll guarantee to take any one at random and train him to become any type of specialist I might select--doctor, lawyer, artist, merchant-chief, and, yes, even beggar man and thief, regardless of his talents, penchants, tendencies, abilities, vocations, and race of his ancestors" (Watson, n.d., p.82).

Children learn from adults they trust by mainly copying from them. Therefore, anxious parents can pass on their behaviors to their offspring. Here are a few things anxious parents may teach their children without even realizing:

- **To avoid taking risks.** This is equivalent to killing the ability of your children to learn new things. How will they ever learn to interact successfully with their environment without taking risks? This is like indirectly putting a child into a maximum security prison, and they cannot thrive.
- **Do not trust other people.**
- **Stay at home, and avoid meeting and interacting with strangers as they may hurt you.**
- **Be scared of uncertainty.** Think about it. How do you get to do new things without facing and handling uncertainty? The growth of a person is related to how much they are willing to navigate unchartered territories.

Unfortunately, some highly anxious parents don't perceive themselves as anxious, and they believe that they think and act from facts. Sadly, there is nothing further from the truth. Even people without anxiety are not always to the point about their own behaviors. If you happen to have been raised by anxious parents, don't hold a grudge against them. They did the best that they knew how. The best you can do is to look, with expectancy, ahead of you and work to handle your anxiety and live a healthy, joyous life. This book contains the ideas and practices that you can implement to begin to turn your life around.

Chapter 3: What to Do to Stay On Top of Your Mental Health

It's vital to realize and understand that everything that happens in your life does so because of your mental consent. This may have occurred while you were still a toddler, an adolescent, or an adult. The reason for this conclusion is pretty basic; most of what you know and believe to be true came through your senses, and over time, it conditioned you into the kind of person that you are today.

If you want to live a healthy, joyous, and exciting life, then it's your primary duty to turn your life around. This is what this chapter will help you do.

Know Yourself

Most of us erroneously believe that we are our thoughts, emotions, and behaviors. Yet, we often say statements like, "My body." Now, who is the "My" saying "my body?" Think about that for a moment. Most people go through their full lives without ever asking this fundamental question. If the body is mine, then I'm not the body. If my mind is mine, then I'm not the mind. All these are the tools I use to live life on this beautiful planet. So, if you're not mind, body, or actions, then you must be something that is invisible. Hence, we say you're a spirit living in a physical body and capable of thinking.

To know yourself simply means to find out what your current personality is. How do you do that? Well, the best tool for that purpose is called self-analysis. After you've done serious introspection, you'll become aware of the kind of person you are and can figure out how to adjust yourself into a happy and healthy individual. Here are three things to do to identify the kind of person you are.

- **Figure out what your six major values are.** Values are nothing but the things and qualities that are non-negotiable in your life. Examples of values include: family, integrity, and care.

- **What are your strengths?** This is important because you may be playing in a field where you're not skilled to excel and feeling bad about it. I don't mean that you can't do anything new; you can. Becoming aware of what you are good at and focusing on that can free you into being one of the creative people in the world.
- **What are your main interests?** Like the strengths above, interests offer a guiding hand to you so that you can do what matters most to you. What's the point of trying to become an online entrepreneur when the thought of online marketing numbs your creativity and de-energizes you?
- **Do you have self-control?**
- **Are you persistent enough to get what you make up your mind to go after?**

When you have figured out the kind of person you are, it may be a ripe time to figure out what your major life purpose is. Have you ever thought about that? This is the one element that all happy and successful people place at the center of their lives. It helps them direct their focus to things that matter most in their lives rather than on things others may want them to do. It also helps avoid turning the clock backwards to thoughts that can trigger anxiety. Viktor Frankl, while in the German concentration camp, observed that "A man who let himself decline because he could not see any future goal found himself occupied with retrospective thoughts" (Frankl, 1984, p.92). Immediately, you decide what your major life goal is; you'll discover that there are certain qualities you'll need to develop to achieve it. Thus, you'll begin to live from inside to the outwards unlike most people who live primarily from the outside to inside. Sadhguru once observed, "The only thing that stands between you and your well-being is a simple fact: you have allowed your thoughts and emotions to take instruction from the outside rather than the inside" (Sadhguru, 2016, p.29).

Now, it's time to learn how to change your habits.

Changing Your Habits

You cannot change your habits until you figure out your reason behind the change. Most people approach this task haphazardly. Decide right now what habit you want to alter and why. Think about how your life will change once you live this new habit. One of the most terrible habits that play a major role in anxiety and fear is the habit of reacting instead of responding. When you react, the external stimulus controls you; while, when responding, you're in charge of whatever is happening. Reacting is really about letting instincts run the show and is normally accompanied by negative emotions and the willingness to take revenge. On the other hand, responding happens after you've given a thought before saying anything. When a stimulus is fired at you, there's a micro moment you can take to think and then to respond.

To illustrate how to alter your habits, we'll assume you want to be in the habit of responding as opposed to reacting so that you can manage anxiety. How do you make the change?

We use a technique that is called self-suggestion. Sometimes, this method of changing your own habits is called autosuggestion. Essentially, instead of allowing external stimuli to enter your ripe mind, you generate your own. We'll couple this process with a technique to help you respond while building this new habit so that you can see the benefits immediately.

Here's a three-step formula to change the reacting habit which you should repeat at least twice daily for a minimum of 90 days:

- **Sit comfortably on a chair and be still and quiet.** This step allows your mind to enter into a receptive state.
- **Take a brief, but a phrase rich with emotion and repeat it over and over for five minutes or so.** You can create any relevant phrase you want, but let me give you one you may begin with. Here it goes: "I'm happy and excited now that I respond to people instead of reacting. I feel good and others enjoy it when I'm in control. Thank you." Say this statement slowly and with feeling, and you'll notice your

feelings change for the better. The best time to do this exercise is early in the morning immediately you wake up and just before retiring to sleep in the evening.
- **Now, see with your mind's eye (while relaxed and eyes closed) your loved ones congratulating you on having become a person with self-control.** Notice the scene where these congratulatory messages are occurring. Pay attention to how you feel.

Now, while altering your reacting habit, practice doing the following each time another person says something that hurts you:
- **Resolve to take two to three breaths before answering back.** Doing this gives you time to evaluate what was said. Never pay too much attention to the person who may have said something bad to you. Always try to focus on the message.
- **Now, give a response that you've thought through thoroughly.**

If you practice this for a number of days, you should notice an improvement in the way you deal with others. Perhaps a good way to remember the above two steps is to write them on a 5x5 card and read them a number of times during the day. If you keep doing so, they'll eventually percolate into the subconscious mind.

What we have said above is a general way that you can use to alter pretty much every habit that you want to change.

How to Handle Fear

In Chapter 1, we saw that the amygdala is the brain area that triggers fear feelings within the human body. The origin of the fear stimulus could be your own thoughts and emotional memories or an external threat such as a snake. Your own thoughts have the power to create an imaginary threat that quickly enters the body into a fear state. Usually, negative thoughts you generate are the culprit and affect the body and the brain. These negative thoughts weaken the immune system and open the way for illness.

Learning to handle negative thoughts is vital because it helps you maintain your health and also to do things that can enhance your life and bring joy. Here are ways to handle fear.

How to Annihilate Negative Thoughts

The only thing that you need to kill negative thoughts successfully using this method is self-awareness, the ability to watch what happens in your mind and body. If you don't have any physical damage to any of your mental faculties, then this will be simple although it might not be easy if it is not yet a habit of yours.

- Identify the event or object that causes you the emotion of fear.
- Turn the searchlight within and spot the automatic thoughts that are flooding your mind.
- Once identified, give a name to the thought. In many cases, once you give a label to the thought it loses its grip over you. But, ensure it is the thought that triggered your fear.
- Now, this is most important, smile and talk back to the negative thought as if it were a person, and that should murder it immediately. If your fear stems from freezing when you're supposed to speak to a group, you may say a statement like this, "I know that I have important ideas to share with these people that I love so much. You're not going to stop me from doing this because these people are more important to me than you are. Leave me alone to enjoy my talk. Thank you."

Essentially, to wrestle the control of your mind from negative thoughts you must realize that you don't have to accept and believe every thought that springs up in your mind.

Learn to Relax Your Body

Most people sleep every evening and some even take a nap during the day. Why do we sleep? We do this for no other reason but to relax the body so that it becomes energized. Also, sleep helps us clear the fog in our minds and helps us to think better. A relaxed body will result in lower blood pressure, reduced anxiety, and improved self-control. This should tell you how important it is to relax your body and mind. But, how do you relax your body and mind? Here's one way that I recommend:

- Find a quiet place where you can be by yourself for about 20 to 30 minutes, and sit in a comfortable chair with your feet on the ground and spine erect.
- Take ten deep, slow breaths. This will help you calm the body down rather quickly.
- Allow thoughts to visit your mind, but don't focus on the negative type. Remember that what you give your energy to tends to grow and become bigger.

The aim of the exercise above is simply to help relax your body, and your mind will follow. As you do this exercise over and over, your amygdala will learn that you're in control and come to respond to your bidding.

Controlling Your Breath

There are certain ways that help calm you down and reduce your pulse and heart rate. Repeated breathing exercises eventually reset your normal breathing and pulse rates; and thus, they will enable you to think clearer. One of the biggest challenges anxious people face is a run-away mind, and breathing can help stop that from happening. The purpose of breath is primarily to take in sufficient oxygen into the body and release as much of the toxic gases as is possible. But, it also helps you manage anxiety if you can do it while it begins to occur. There are several breathing techniques you can do, but I'll share with you just one method you can practice right away.

Belly breathing

Most of us breathe primarily from the chest. Unfortunately, there's very little movement in the rib cage because it is rigid. But, there's a strong muscle between the belly and the rib cage that you

can manipulate to increase the volumes of the lungs. You may also use it to squeeze the carbon dioxide-laden air out of your body. This is how you go about stomach breathing:
- Sit comfortably on a chair, and erect your spine.
- Place your right hand on your tummy and your left hand on your chest, and breathe. Adjust your breathing until you almost exclusively breathe from the belly.
- Take deep breaths by expanding your stomach as much as is possible. Then, exhale slowly for as long as you can. That should expel most of the bad gasses out of your body.

That's all there is to belly breathing. Practice this exercise at least twice a day and soon it will become a habit and a good habit at that.

Improve Your Self-Confidence

The beginning of improving your self-confidence is through self-analysis. If you've done the self-analysis exercise that I suggested above, you may have realized that you're not a bad person. Yes, you may have some deficiencies, but almost everyone lacks at least one quality that blocks them from being the best they can be. Napoleon Hill once studied over 500 of America's wealthiest men and discovered that all of them had self-confidence at the back of their sails. He once wrote, "Self-confidence is the product of knowledge. Know yourself, know how much you know (and how little), why you know it, and how you are going to use it" (Hill, 1928, p.68). I agree with this late philosopher that when you know yourself, your self-confidence spikes, and you set yourself up to deal with life's challenges such as fear and anxiety.

Self-confidence is about having faith in yourself and abilities to overcome challenges, including emotions such as fear. The most potent weapon to use to build the kind of self-confidence that you want is called self-suggestion. The reason this weapon is powerful is because it mimics how we learnt everything that we positively know such as riding a bicycle. Before you begin with building self-confidence, picture in your mind the kind of person you wish to become. What would this person do if they weren't afraid? How does this person run their day-to-day activities? How do they relate to others? As you know, you cannot successfully complete a task unless there's a strong motive behind it; hence, the questions I've posed here are relevant.

Now that you have an idea of the kind of person you want to become insofar as self-confidence is concerned, it's time to program your subconscious mind with this new image of yourself. Here's how to go about it:

- Sit comfortably and relax your body, and also quiet your mind. The purpose is to render your mind receptive to the suggestion that's coming.
- Now, read the following creed aloud so that you can hear yourself, and do so with feeling: "I know that I was created with all the tools I need to live a full and enjoyable life. I also know that I was brought on this beautiful planet to win at what I do. Therefore, I persistently act daily with confidence so that my life is pleasant and joyous. I am aware that my dominating thoughts eventually become my habitual way of doing things. So, I always focus my mind on thoughts that lead me to act confidently and live a fear-free life. Thank you." Ensure that you read this statement daily for at least 90 consecutive days. If you miss one day, start afresh to count your 90 days. This period is enough to replace your habitual fear thoughts with confidence and thus be able to prevent anxiety even before it begins.

How to Handle a Panic Attack

A panic attack is an intense anxiety that triggers trembling, chest pain, hyperventilating, or elevated heart rate. Gary once went to see Dr. Amen several years ago after having seen his physician with a sore back. After investigating, the doctor had detected a soft spot over Gary's kidney. He then asked Gary to take a kidney x-ray. But Gary's thoughts immediately ran wild. He began to think that the physician would discover that he had cancer and be forced to have chemotherapy.

The bad, negative thoughts didn't stop there. Gary went on to think that he'd lose his nice hair, experience massive pain, and then die. All these thoughts took less than a minute, and Gary's heart rate skyrocketed, he started to hyperventilate, and he began to sweat profusely. He was experiencing the physical symptoms of a panic attack. He looked at the doctor and said that he can't get an x-ray. People like Gary tend to have high neural activity in the amygdala areas of their brains and are prone to heavy anxiety. Panic attacks are painful though they last for a few minutes. How, then, do you protect yourself from such scary body reactions brought by intense anxiety?

The major culprit in such cases is the amygdala, and it needs to be taught to differentiate between a real threat and an imagined one. It is times when your fortune-telling, negative thoughts run wild that you should take over the reins of your mind. Doing so helps you control anxiety. Here's a way you can set yourself up to deal with anxiety before it becomes a panic attack:

- **The moment you notice yourself thinking negative thoughts, interrupt them**. You have self-awareness and can watch over conscious activities of your mind. Once you interrupt your thoughts, your body won't show the signs of anxiety because you would have removed the cause.
- **In some cases you may not be able to catch your negative thoughts, so it can speed up the onset of anxiety by increasing your breathing rate**. When this happens, quickly intervene and slow down your breath. This will help you calm your mind and body, and it will rid you of possible anxiety.

To fortify your mind and body to handle anxiety, carry out the steps and processes we suggested above on handling fear. It will be helpful if you add them to your daily repertoire of activities, but make them essential because when your health suffers there's very little else you can accomplish.

It's possible for the exercises that we've suggested to fail to deliver the kind of results you want. In such a case, consider consulting a knowledgeable doctor who knows the science behind fear and anxiety. Perhaps also consider taking brain images to check if your basal ganglia (brain area that includes the amygdala) is not hyperactive. If it is found that it is overly active, medication could help you in the short-term while working on reprogramming your brain for long-term anxiety control.

Conclusion

We've now covered what we promised from the beginning of the book. Now, I want us to create a resource that you can quickly refer to when you want to remember the key ideas discussed in the pages of this book. The way we'll do this is by exhuming the most important ideas discussed in each chapter and place them in this part of the book. It will then be easier for you to quickly access them when necessary.

In chapter 1, we began by differentiating between fear and anxiety. We indicated that fear is an emotional reaction you get when you face an immediate threat such as a bear or lion. On the other hand, we defined anxiety as a feeling that arises when the threat we face is in the future, and it usually originates from our mental activities when directed at negative thoughts. The key brain part that facilitates the body's reaction to these threats is the amygdala. The one key to keep in mind is that the amygdala stores emotional memories which means it can learn new emotions if approached correctly.

The next idea that we covered was the cognitive-behavioral approach to anxiety. This method brings together the understanding of the linkages between thinking and behavior to affect change. However, for lasting change, the source of thoughts that activate the amygdala must be altered to experience a lasting change. This source is our beliefs. I'm talking here about core beliefs not the rational beliefs that people often claim to have. These are beliefs that determine the kind of conscious and subconscious thinking that you often do. We also provided the story of the 27-year-old Indian man who used this method to turn around his social life and even take the organization that he worked for to another level.

Chapter 2 focused our attention on anxieties we face at work, social environments, family, and relationships. Focusing on these you'll recognize that you are the center through which these anxieties occur. The beautiful thing is that you're already working on your anxiety and this will spill over into other areas of your life such as work. The most important idea we talked about was the concept of cognitive distortions, the tendency to predict what another person is thinking. We have not yet developed to a point where we can do that with accuracy. So, deal with facts rather than opinions. This goes to handling work, family, social, and relationship anxieties.

The last chapter took us through ways you can take charge of your mental health. The key one is the importance of knowing yourself because everything that happens to you must go through you. That makes you the most important variable in the whole of this book. This, therefore, calls for a thorough analysis of the kind of a person you are. Hence, we've given pointers to get you started in this direction. One other idea we talked about was panic attack. Trying to deal with it when in the midst of the pain is nearly impossible. The best thing to do is to catch yourself while on the path to the attack. That is why self-knowledge is such an important aspect of your mental health. Other valuable ideas that we discussed include self-confidence. This is a quality that enters almost all social settings in your life. When you get it right, things like social anxiety pack their bags and leave your mind and body. I want to end this with words that you should burn in your marvelous mind. If possible, write them on a card, and read them as often as you deem practical, and they'll guide your life whether you're aware of it or not. They are the words of Sadhguru, the Indian mystic, and he once said:

"What then is the way out? The way out is a very simple change in direction. You just need to see that the source and basis of your experience is within you. Human experience may be stimulated or catalyzed by external situations, but the source is within. Pain or pleasure, joy or misery, agony or ecstasy, happens only inside you" (Sadhguru, 2016, p.31).

If You Enjoyed This Book In Anyway, An Honest Review Is Always Appreciated!

www.ingramcontent.com/pod-product-compliance
Lightning Source LLC
Chambersburg PA
CBHW030304030426
42336CB00009B/511